Voice Catcher
an anthology

edited by
Heather Kay

The cover picture is a reproduction of "Lift Off,"
a painting by Barry Jackson

Voice Care Network UK

Published by the
Voice Care Network UK
Registered charity number 1087751

Registered office
29 Southbank Road
Kenilworth CV8 1LA

phone/fax: 01926 864000
email: info@voicecare.org.uk
web site: www.voicecare.org.uk

First published 2008

A catalog record for this book is available from the British Library

ISBN 978-0-9524524-4-7

Printed and bound by Q3 Digital/Litho, Loughborough, Leics. LE11 1LE

FOREWORD

by David Crystal O.B.E., F.B.A.
Honorary Professor of Linguistics, University of Bangor

I love anthologies. I love language. The two rarely come together. I have made the connection myself just once. My wife Hilary and I spent a happy year in 1998-9 combing library shelves looking for quotations about language and languages. Penguin Books published the result the following year: it was called *Words on Words*. We were amazed at the frequency with which authors of all genres and backgrounds sooner or later had something to say about language - whether about listening, speaking, reading, or writing, about its origins, analysis, and evaluation, about accents and dialects, about slang, swearing, and style, and a thousand topics more. But our approach was a minimalist one. We had space only for the shortest of extracts, and we often bemoaned the fact that we could not present our findings in their full glory.

I suppose this regret must have been at the back of my mind when I spoke at the VCN weekend in Winchester, a couple of years later, and we shared a few poems with each other. There was no anthology then to dip into, and pieces were hard to find. Five years on, and I was beginning to think that there would never be one. *Voice Catcher* changes all that.

I make a bet with any reader (apart from the editors). You will not previously have read all the items in this collection. After my *Words on Words* experience, I thought I had read it all. How wrong I was! Many of the pieces in *Voice Catcher* are new to me, and what a delight it has been to read them. I am indebted to the many contributors who have taken the trouble to share their reading in this way, and all praise to the editor and the team who have put this remarkable work together, for I well know just how complex and time-consuming a task it is.

Voice Catcher is a linguistic firework display, sparkling with all the colours of the auditory rainbow. The focus on speaking and listening will make it an invaluable resource for professionals, and the sheer brilliance of the pieces will bring our voiceworld to the attention of a broader public as never before. Talking about a visit to Shakespeare's Stratford, in this collection, Elizabeth Jennings reflects:

"Words aren't worn
Out in this place but can renew our tongue,
Flesh out our feeling, make us apt for life."

Voice Catcher, in its own way, does the same.

INTRODUCTION

L et us all bring a poem to share together after dinner". Thus David Crystal, at a weekend meeting of the VCN, set this Anthology going. A good poem or story, an anecdote or a joke demands an ear. A shared meal helps us to relax into interaction.

"Do you know this one?"

"Listen to this ...."

"Have you heard ...?"

The occasion tapped into a rich vein of hoarded treasures. Once exposed, further pathways opened up as each listener's personal response recalled forgotten poems and rejoiced in new discoveries. We had been emotionally and intellectually stretched, jostled out of our well-worn ruts, and enjoyed laughing together. Any of our gathering of teachers and therapists is always hungry for new ideas and materials that will excite their students, so the powerful stimulus of that evening's entertainment whetted our appetites. We looked forward to the pleasures of browsing with a purpose.

"This reminds me of ..."

"I'd forgotten about ..."

"Where can I find ...?"

"What about prose – plays – conversations?"

The criteria for inclusion in a voice anthology begin to define themselves.

"Does this piece celebrate, describe, explore aspects of the speaking voice or its effects? The variety and power of language? At the same time do the words leap off the page? Arrest the listener, stretch the vocal range, challenge the articulation? Can we use this book?"

Now the ball is rolling!

In fact, fielding the contributions of members of the Voice Care Network from all over the country has been like playing a pinball machine. Some players fire the ball and let it dribble back for another try, others let it fly with noisy bravado only for it to drop straight to the bottom without making any contacts and disappear with a rattle and a groan.

"Too long – too obscure – too literary – already got one by her – well, no more than two then – spread the net wide"

Some nudge up the score by repetitive bouncing as the same offering from different sources clamours to stay in the game. Some reverse unexpectedly or are reprieved at the last minute. But O, the excitement of recognising a direct hit as the screen lights up with noisy jubilation! Congratulations to the contributing players for ringing so many bells! Coming from different areas of the voice care territory you have extended its parameters. The Anthology takes on a life of its own and turns out to be more than a collection of writings that celebrate voices and languages, speech and the need to tell. It is also, of course, about feelings and emotions and how words fail or are unstoppable and how voices can be imprisoned or excessive and about listening and the need of the heart for silence. So here it is – a diverse catch of voices harvested by a Network.

Perhaps this is one of its particular characteristics, and another is the fact that it originated from a live entertainment. I hope the book still retains some of the immediacy and relaxed enjoyment of that occasion. The passage from there to here has inevitably involved much discussion, sounding out, researching, tracking down, brooding.

Many have shared these activities but it is in the nature of all working parties that they eventually shrink into a dedicated crew. You would not be holding this book now were it not for the Voice Catcher crew, who, keeping a look-out for hazards and landmarks, taking soundings, checking the compass bearings and by tying up or fending off, backed up the skipper in plotting and navigating the course. The skipper's log book entries record the stalwart deck work by Val, Roz, David and the bosun - Annabel.

We think it important that each piece should stand alone on a page and be allowed to make its own impact without pre-empted expectations from its neighbours. However, for ease of working and for sparking off other ideas, we let them find their own resonances and group themselves into loose sections – which is how they appear in the Contents. None are permanently tethered and could migrate.

I hope you will be inspired to make your own connexions, rearrange and add to these ingredients. So help yourself, enjoy the feast and cook up your own menus!

Heather Kay

CONTENTS

1. In the beginning . . .

2. "the need of the throat and tongue for speech"

3. The need of the heart for silence

4. "Yes the highest things are beyond words"

9. Talk Proper

10. Get your tongue round that

The Little Mute Boy

The little boy was looking for his voice.
(The king of the crickets had it.)
In a drop of water
the little boy was looking for his voice

I do not want it for speaking with;
I will make a ring of it
that my silence may wear
on its little finger

In a drop of water
the little boy was looking for his voice

(The captive voice, far away,
put on a cricket's clothes.)

Federico Garcia Lorca
(Translated by WS Merwin)

A poem is

something that someone is saying
no louder, Pip, than my 'goodnight'-
words with a tune, which outstaying
their speaker travel as far
as that amazing, vibrant light
from a long-extinguished star

Jon Stallworthy

From **Birds of Heaven**

We began before words, and we will end beyond them.

It sometimes seems to me that our days are poisoned with too many words. Words said and not meant. Words said *and* meant. Words divorced from feeling. Wounding words. Words that conceal. Words that reduce. Dead words.

If only words were a kind of fluid that collects in the ears, if only they turned into the visible chemical equivalent of their true value, an acid, or something curative — then we might be more careful. Words do collect in us anyway. They collect in the blood, in the soul, and either transform or poison people's lives. Bitter or thoughtless words poured into the ears of the young have blighted many lives in advance. We all know people whose unhappy lives twist on a set of words uttered to them on a certain unforgotten day at school, in childhood, or at university.

…A bump on the head may pass away, but a cutting remark grows with the mind…we know all too well the awesome power of words…we use them with such deadly and accurate cruelty.

We are all wounded inside in some way…We all carry unhappiness within us…Which is why we need a little gentleness and healing from one another. Healing in words, and healing beyond words. Like gestures. Warm gestures. Like friendship, which will always be a mystery. Like a smile, which someone described as the shortest distance between two people.

Yes the highest things are beyond words…

I think we need more of the wordless in our lives. We need more stillness, more of a sense of wonder, a feeling for the mystery of life.

We need more love, more silence, more deep listening, more deep giving.

Ben Okri

Aphasia

I'M SEVEN, and I'm dead bright,
But words give me a fright.
Words are bullies.
Sneaky things. They gabble and lie.
Sometimes trying to understand
Them makes me cry. Words hurt.
Words are all over the place.
They get shoved in my face.
I don't know why but
Words make me cry.

I wish words were things
You could hug,
Or that they smelt nice.
I wish they came in bottles
Like fizzy-drinks, or melted
Like ice-cream. But they don't.
Words are mean. They bully me.
Lock me away
From what I want to say.

I can't even ask for help,
And I'm only seven
(And a bit).
Words spread nasty gossip.
They must. Otherwise why
Would people think I'm thick?

Words,
They make me sick
Inside.

Brian Patten

The Word

The word
was born in the blood,
grew in the dark body, beating,
and flew through the lips and the mouth

Further away and nearer
still, still it came
from dead fathers and from wandering races,
from lands that had returned to stone,
weary of their poor tribes,
because when pain took to the roads,
the settlements set out and arrived
and new lands and water reunited
to sow their word anew.
And so, this is the inheritance -
this is the wavelength which connects us
with the dead man and the dawn
of new beings not yet come to light.

Still the atmosphere quivers
with the initial word
dressed up
in terror and sighing.
It emerged
from the darkness
and until now there is not thunder
that rumbles yet with all the iron
of that word,
the first
word uttered -
perhaps it was only a ripple, a drop,
and yet its great cataract falls and falls.

Later on, the word fills with meaning.
It remained gravid and it filled up with lives.
Everything had to do with births and sounds -
affirmation, clarity, strength,
negation, destruction, death -
the verb took over all the power
and blended existence with essence
in the electricity of its beauty.

Pablo Neruda
(Translated by Alastair Reid)

I am the Song

I am the song that sings the bird.
I am the leaf that grows the land.
I am the tide that moves the moon.
I am the stream that halts the sand.
I am the cloud that drives the storm.
I am the earth that lights the sun.
I am the fire that strikes the stone.
I am the clay that shapes the hand.
I am the word that speaks the man.

Charles Causley

Child Development

As sure as prehistoric fish grew legs
and sauntered off the beaches into forests
working up some irregular verbs for their
first conversation, so three-year-old children
enter the phase of name-calling.

Every day a new one arrives and is added
to the repertoire. You Dumb Goopyhead,
You Big Sewerface, You Poop-on-the-Floor
(a kind of Navaho ring to that one)
they yell from knee level,
their little mugs flushed with challenge.
Nothing Samuel Johnson would bother tossing out
in a pub, but then the toddlers are not trying
to devastate some fatuous Enlightenment hack.

They are just tormenting their fellow squirts
or going after the attention of the giants
way up there with their cocktails and bad breath
talking baritone nonsense to other giants,
waiting to call them names after thanking
them for the lovely party and hearing the door close.

The mature save their hothead invective
for things: an errant hammer, tire chains,
or receding trains missed by seconds,
though they know in their adult hearts,
even as they threaten to banish Timmy to bed
for his appalling behavior,
that their bosses are Big Fatty Stupids,
their wives are Dopey Dopeheads
and that they themselves are Mr Sillypants.

Billy Collins

The Whisperer

For twenty months I whispered,
  Spoke aloud
  Not one word,
Except when the doctor, checking my chest, said:
  'Say Ninety-nine',
  And, from the mine
Of my throat, hauling up my voice like a load of metal, I
  Said 'Ninety-nine.'
  From sixteen-
years-old to my eighteenth birthday I whispered clock
  And season round;
  Made no sound
More than the wind that entered without knocking
  Through the door
  That wasn't there
Or the slid-wide window that un-shuttered half the wall of my
  Shepherd's bothy
  Of a chalet.
In the hushed sanatorium night I coughed in whispers
  To stray cats
  And dogs that
Stalked in from the forest fogs to the warmth of my anthracite stove,
  And at first light
  Of shrill July
To the robin winding its watch beside spread trays of cedars.
  Day after day
  My larynx lay
In dry dock until whispering seemed
  The normal way
  Of speaking: I
Was surprised at the surprise on the face of strangers
  Who wondered why
  I was so shy.
When I talked to next-bed neighbours, out-of-breath on the
  Gravel track,
  They whispered back
As if the practice were infectious. Garrulous as a budgie,
  I filled the air
  Of my square

Thermometered and Lysolled cage with the agitated
       Wheezes, squeaks
       And wind-leaks
Of my punctured Northumbrian pipes. And when the doctor
         asked me
       How I felt, 'I'm
       Feeling fine',
I whispered—my temperature down to thirty-seven,
       The sore grate
       Soothed from my throat,
And all the winds of Hampshire to ventilate my lungs.

Two winters went whispered away before I ventured
       Out of my cage,
       Over the hedge,
On to the chalky chines, the sparse, pony-trodden,
        adder-ridden
       Grass. Alone
       Among pine
Trunks I whispered comfortable sermons to
       Congregations
       Of worms. Patients
On exercise in copse or on common, sighting me
       At distance, gave
       Me a wave,
And I in reply blew a blast on my police-
       man's whistle,
       Meaning: 'Listen.
Wait! Come closer. I've something to tell.'
       But when tea-
       time brought me
To drawing-room and chatter, the thunder of shook cups,
       Crack of laughter,
       Stunned and baffled
Me. I bawled in whispers four-inch from the ear
       Of him or her
       Unheeded. Words,
Always unheard, failed even articulate me.
       Frantic, I'd rap
       Table or clap

Hands, crying: 'Listen, for God's sake listen!' And suddenly the room
          Fell silent,
          Waiting, and I
Words failing again, fell silent too.
                              The world moved
          Noisily on.
          My larynx soon
Was afloat again but my life still drifts in whispers.
          I shout out loud
          To no crowd,
Straining to be heard above its strangling murmur, but
          Look for one face
          Lit with the grace
Of listening, the undeadened brow that marks an undeafened
          Ear. I try
          To catch an eye;
Nod, nudge, wink, beckon, signal with clicked
          Fingers, roll
          Words to a ball
And toss them for the wind to play with. Life roars round me like
          A dynamo.
          I stump, stamp, blow
Whistle over and over, staring into the rowdy air, seeking
          You or you,
          Anyone who
Can lip-read the words of my whisper as clear as the clang of a bell,
          Can see me say:
          'Wait! Wait!
          Come closer;
          I've something to tell.'

Norman Nicholson

Prayer before Birth

I am not yet born; O hear me.
Let not the bloodsucking bat or the rat or the stoat or the
    club-footed ghoul come near me.

I am not yet born, console me.
I fear that the human race may with tall walls wall me,
    with strong drugs dope me, with wise lies lure me,
        on black racks rack me, in blood-baths roll me.

I am not yet born; provide me
With water to dandle me, grass to grow for me, trees to talk
    to me, sky to sing to me, birds and a white light
        in the back of my mind to guide me.

I am not yet born; forgive me
For the sins that in me the world shall commit, my words
    when they speak me, my thoughts when they think me,
        my treason engendered by traitors beyond me,
            my life when they murder by means of my
                hands, my death when they live me.

I am not yet born; rehearse me
In the parts I must play and the cues I must take when
    old men lecture me, bureaucrats hector me, mountains
        frown at me, lovers laugh at me, the white
            waves call me to folly and the desert calls
                me to doom and the beggar refuses
                    my gift and my children curse me.

I am not yet born; O hear me,
Let not the man who is beast or who thinks he is God
    come near me.

I am not yet born; O fill me
With strength against those who would freeze my
    humanity, would dragoon me into a lethal automaton,
        would make me a cog in a machine, a thing with
            one face, a thing, and against all those
                who would dissipate my entirety, would
                    blow me like thistledown hither and
                      thither or hither and thither
                      like water held in the
                        hands would spill me.

Let them not make me a stone and let them not spill me.
Otherwise kill me.

Louis MacNeice

From **Mundo and the Weather Child**

The book begins with a description of a child celebrating his seventh birthday. He is given a bag of marbles, a present he loves. All day he plays with them experimenting with the sound they make when rattled, tipped or rolled. That night he sleeps and has a dreadful dream...
The story is a first hand account.

'I was trapped inside a marble, like a coloured swirl, unable to move or cry out. My parents searched the room for me, turning over the bedclothes, looking under the bed and in my wardrobe, emptying the drawers. All the time I was staring at them from the floor in the corner of my room where I had rolled inside the marble, tiny and petrified, my cries frozen into silence. But they didn't look, didn't see, left me there, so cold and so alone.'

The child develops a fever, is seriously ill and, as a result, becomes profoundly deaf and describes it thus . . .

'I was trapped inside a prison that no one could see or feel, yet which not a sound could enter. Outside the prison, crying to be admitted, was *my* voice, my *own* voice, so why couldn't I hear it?

Why had the world gone silent? Why were my cries swallowed up? I felt nothing so simple as pain, only suddenly very lost. Deaf? There wasn't a voice I could hear to tell me what that meant.

Later I was taken to see a stranger who sat in a darkened room amongst mysterious points of light. He wore a white mask over his face and had a great silver dial strapped to his forehead, which he flashed onto my face. Tapping a double-pronged wand on his knee he pressed it hard against my earbone. Robed attendants stood around.

"He is a wizard," I thought, "and this is still a bad dream. Soon I shall wake up."

Soon came and soon went but I didn't wake up. There was a second visit to the wizard and another wizard was called in. They had earphones and machinery and poked instruments into my ears. Then they solemnly shook their heads. They had no spells that worked and my prison remained intact. I couldn't get out and no one else could get in. There were no doors, no windows, not even a pinhole or a tiny crack, through which a voice might find its way.

I couldn't hear a thing!'

Joyce Dunbar

The Mouth

I went to the mirror
but the mirror was bare,
looked for my mouth
but my mouth wasn't there.
Over the lips had grown
a whiskered hymen of skin.

I went to the window
wanting to shout
I pictured the words
but nothing came out.
The face beneath the nose
an empty hoarding.

And as I waited, I could feel
flesh filling in the space behind.
Teeth melted away tasting of snow
as the stalactites of the palate
joined the stalagmites below.
The tongue, like a salted snail,
sweated and shrivelled.

The doctor has suggested plastic surgery:
a neat incision, cosmetic dentistry
and full red lips.
He meant well but I declined.

After all, there are advantages.
At last I have given up smoking,
and though food is a needle
twice a day, it needs no cooking.
There is little that I miss.
I never could whistle and there's no one to kiss.

In the street, people pass by
unconcerned. I give no one directions
and in return am given none.
When asked if I am happy
I look the inquisitor straight in the eye
and think to myself ...("

Roger McGough

The gift of speech

He spoke:
his round mouth open
and shut in the manner
of a fish's song.
A bubbling hiss
could be heard
as the void
rushed headlong
like marsh gas.

Miroslav Holub
(translated by Ewald Osers)

Not love perhaps

This is not Love perhaps – love that lays down
Its life, that many waters cannot quench, not the floods drown-
But something written in lighter ink, said in a lower-tone:
Something perhaps especially on our own:
A need at times to be together and talk —
And then the finding we can walk
More firmly through dark narrow places
And meet more easily nightmare faces:
A need to reach out sometimes hand to hand-
And then find Earth less like an alien land:
A need for alliance to defeat
The whisperers at the corner of the street:
A need for inns on roads, islands in seas, halls for discoveries to be shared,
Maps checked and notes compared:
A need at times of each for each
Direct as the need of throat & tongue for speech.

A.J.S Tessimond

Richard II Act I Scene 3 Mowbray

MOWBRAY
> A heavy sentence, my most sovereign liege,
> And all unlooked for from your highness' mouth.
> A dearer merit, not so deep a maim
> As to be cast forth in the common air,
> Have I deserved at your highness' hands.
> The language I have learnt these forty years,
> My native English, now I must forgo,
> And now my tongue's use is to me no more
> Than an unstringed viol or a harp,
> Or like a cunning instrument cased up —
> Or being open, put into his hands
> That knows no touch to tune the harmony.
> Within my mouth you have engaoled my tongue,
> Doubly portcullised with my teeth and lips,
> And dull unfeeling barren ignorance
> Is made my gaoler to attend on me.
> I am too old to fawn upon a nurse,
> Too far in years to be a pupil now.
> What is thy sentence then but speechless death,
> Which robs my tongue from breathing native breath?

William Shakespeare

Second Language

English not being yet a language, I wrapped my lubber-lips
    around my thumb;
Brain-deaf as an embryo, I was snuggled in my comfort-
    blanket dumb.

Growling figures campaniled above me, and twanged their
    carillons of bronze
Sienna consonants embedded with the vowels *alexandrite,*
    emerald and *topaz.*

The topos of their discourse seemed to do with me and
    convoluted genealogy;
Wordy whorls and braids and skeins and spiral helices,
    unskeletoned from laminate geology —

How this one's slate-blue gaze is correspondent to
    another's new-born eyes;
Gentians, forget-me-nots, and cornflowers, diurnal in a
    heliotrope surmise.

Alexandrine tropes came gowling out like beagles, loped and
    and unroped
On a snuffly Autumn. Nimrod followed after with his bold
    Arapahoes,

Who whooped and hollered in their unforked tongue. The trail
    was starred with
Myrrh and frankincense of Anno Domini; the Wise Men
    wisely paid their tariff.

A single star blazed at my window. Crepuscular, its acoustic
    perfume dims
And swells like flowers on the stanzaic-papered wall.
    Shipyard hymns

Then echoed from the East: gantry-clank and rivet-ranks, Six-
    County hexametric
Brackets, bulkheads, girders, beams, and stanchions;
    convocated and Titanic.

Leviathans of rope snarled out from ropeworks: disgorged
hawsers, unkinkable lay,
Ratlines, S-twists, plaited halyards, Z-twists, catlines; all had
their say.

Tobacco-scent and snuff breathed out in gouts of factory
smoke like aromatic camomile;
Sheaves of brick-built mill-stacks glowered in the sulphur-
mustard fog like campaniles.

The dim bronze noise of midnight-noon and Angelus then
boomed and clinked in Latin
Conjugations; statues wore their shrouds of amaranth; the
thurible chinked out its smoky patina.

I inhaled *amo, amas, amat* in quids of *pros* and *versus* and
Introibos
Ad altare Dei; incomprehensibly to others, spoke in Irish. I
slept through the Introit.

The enormous Monastery surrounded me with nave and
architrave. Its ornate pulpit
Spoke to me in fleurs-de-lys of Purgatory. Its sacerdotal gaze
became my pupil.

My pupil's nose was bathed in Pharaonic unguents of dope and
glue.
Flimsy tissue-paper plans of aeroplanes unfolded whimsical
ideas of the blue,

Where, unwound, the prop's elastic is unpropped and balsa-
wood extends its wings
Into the hazardous azure of April. It whirrs into the realm of
things.

Things are kinks that came in tubes; like glue or paint
extruded, that became
A hieroglyphic alphabet. Incestuous in pyramids, Egyptians
were becalmed.

I climbed into it, delved its passageways, its sepulchral
interior, its things of kings
Embalmed; sarcophagi, whose perfume I exhumed in chancy
versions of the *I-Ching*.

A chink of dawn was revelated by the window. Far-off cocks
    crowed crowingly
And I woke up, verbed and tensed with speaking English; I
    lisped the words so knowingly.

I love the as-yet morning, when no one's abroad, and I am like
    a postman on his walk,
Distributing strange messages and bills, and arbitrations with
    the world of talk:

I foot the snow and almost-dark. My shoes are crisp, and bite
    into the blue-
White firmament of pavement. My father holds my hand and
    goes blah-

Blah with me into the ceremonial dawn. I'm wearing tweed.
    The universe is Lent
And Easter is an unspun cerement, the gritty, knitty, tickly
    cloth of unspent

Time. I feel its warp and weft. Bobbins pirn and shuttle in
    Imperial
Typewriterspeak. I hit the keys. The ribbon-black clunks out
    the words in serial.

What comes next is next, and no one knows the *che sera* of it,
    but must allow
The *Tipp-Ex* present at the fingertips. Listen now: an angel
    whispers of the here-and-now.

The future looms into the mouth incessantly, gulped-at and
    unspoken;
Its guardian is intangible, but gives you hints and winks and
    nudges as its broken token.

I woke up blabbering and dumb with too much sleep. I rubbed
    my eyes and ears.
I closed my eyes again and flittingly, forgetfully, I glimpsed
    the noise of years.

Ciaran Carson

Hindi Urdu Bol Chaal

(*bol chaal:* dialogue)

These are languages I try to touch
as if my tongue is a fingertip gently
matching its whorls to echoings of sound.

Separating Urdu from Hindi—it's like
sifting grains of wild rice
or separating India from Pakistan.

The sign of nasal intonation
floats like a heat haze
above new words.

Words like hands banging on the table.

*

I introduce myself to two languages,
but there are so many—of costume,
of conduct and courtesy.

I listen hard as if to sense minute
changes of dialect from village to village
from West Punjab to West Bengal.

These languages could have been mine—
the whisper of silks on silks
And the slapping and patting of chapattis on the tava.

*

I imagine the meetings and greetings
in Urdu borrowed from Sanskrit,
Arabic and Persian.

I shall be borrowed from England,
Pakistan, assalaam alaikum —-
Peace be with you — Helloji.

It is not you I am meeting.
It is a sound system travelling through
countries, ascending and descending

in ragas, drumbeats, clapping.

*

In Lahore there grows a language tree
its roots branching to an earlier time
its fruit ripe, ready to fall.

I hear the rustling of mango groves
my living and dead relatives
quarrelling together and I search

for a nugget of sound, the kernel
of language. I am enlarged
by what I cannot hear —-

the village conferences, the crackling
of bonfires and the rap of gunfire.

*

My senses stir with words
that must be reinvented.
At the market I'll ask *How much?*

and wait for just one new word
to settle like a stone
at the bottom of a well.

Moniza Alvi

21

The Tempest Act I Scene 2 Miranda

MIRANDA   Abhorrèd slave,
Which any print of goodness wilt not take,
Being capable of all ill! I pitied thee,
Took pains to make thee speak, taught thee each hour
One thing or other. When thou didst not, savage,
Know thine own meaning, but wouldst gabble like
A thing most brutish, I endowed thy purposes
With words that made them known. But thy vile race,
Though thou didst learn, had that in't which good natures
Could not abide to be with; therefore wast thou
Deservedly confined into this rock,
Who hadst deserved more than a prison.

CALIBAN   You taught me language, and my profit on't
Is I know how to curse. The red plague rid you
For learning me your language!

William Shakespeare

A mantra for you — and for me

As far as you can ...be yourself.
Say your truth in words of your choosing.

Listen to others; no one is always fluent,
always knowing and saying the right word.

Command your own space
and speak your own piece
and tell your own story.

And if you stumble,
don't feel alone and don't be downcast.
Little by little, let your words be heard.

People will listen ...
and will want to know more of you.

David Preece

Listening

You are not listening to me when . .

> You do not care about me;
> You say you understand me before you know me well enough;
> You have an answer to my problem before I've finished telling you
> what my problem is;
> You cut me off before I've finished speaking;
> You finish my sentence for me;
> You find me boring;
> You feel critical of my vocabulary, grammar or accent;
> You are dying to tell me something;
> You tell me about your experience, making mine seem unimportant;
> You are communicating to someone else in the room;
> You refuse my thanks, saying you haven't really done anything;
> You follow your own thoughts and memories when they are
> triggered by my words.

You are listening to me when ... .

> You come quietly into my private world and let me be;
> You really try to fully understand me, even if I am not making much
> sense;
> You grasp my point of view even when it's against your sincere
> convictions;
> You allow me the dignity of making my own decisions even though
> you think they might be wrong;
> You do not take my problem from me, but allow me to deal with it
> in my own way;
> You hold back your desire to give me good advice;
> You give me enough room to discover for myself what is really going
> on;
> You accept my gift of gratitude by telling me how good it makes you
> feel to know you have been helpful.

Anon

Not now, Bernard

'Hello, Dad,' said Bernard.
'Not now, Bernard,' said his father.
'Hello, Mum,' said Bernard.
'Not now, Bernard,' said his mother.
'There's a monster in the garden and it's going to eat me,'
said Bernard.
'Not now, Bernard,' said his mother.
Bernard went into the garden.
'Hello, Monster,' he said to the monster.
The monster ate Bernard up, every bit.
Then the monster went indoors.
'ROAR,' went the monster behind Bernard's mother.
'Not now, Bernard,' said Bernard's mother.
The monster bit Bernard's father.
'Not now, Bernard,' said Bernard's father.
'Your dinner's ready,' said Bernard's mother.
She put the dinner in front of the television.
The monster ate the dinner.
Then it watched the television.
Then it read one of Bernard's comics.
And broke one of his toys.
'Go to bed. I've taken up your milk,' called Bernard's mother.
The monster went upstairs.
'But I'm a monster,' said the monster.
'Not now, Bernard,' said Bernard's mother.

David McKee

The Voice

Safe in the magic of my woods
    I lay, and watched the dying light.
Faint in the pale high solitudes,
    And washed with rain and veiled by night,

Silver and blue and green were showing.
    And the dark woods grew darker still;
And birds were hushed; and peace was growing;
    And quietness crept up the hill;

And no wind was blowing . . .

And I knew
That this was the hour of knowing,
And the night and the woods and you
Were one together, and I should find
Soon in the silence the hidden key
Of all that had hurt and puzzled me—
Why you were you, and the night was kind,
And the woods were part of the heart of me.

And there I waited breathlessly,
Alone; and slowly the holy three,
The three that I loved, together grew
One, in the hour of knowing,
Night, and the woods, and you———

And suddenly
There was an uproar in my woods,
The noise of a fool in mock distress,
Crashing and laughing and blindly going,
Of ignorant feet and a swishing dress,
And a Voice profaning the solitudes.

The spell was broken, the key denied me,
And at length your flat clear voice beside me
Mouthed cheerful clear flat platitudes.

You came and quacked beside me in the wood.
You said, 'The view from here is very good !'
You said, 'It's nice to be alone a bit !'
And, 'How the days are drawing out!' you said.
You said, 'The sunset's pretty, isn't it ?'

       *   *   *

By God! I wish—I wish that you were dead!

Rupert Brooke

Talk

I wish people, when you sit near them,
Wouldn't feel it necessary to make conversation
And send thin draughts of words
Blowing down you neck and your ears
And giving you a cold in your inside.

D.H.Lawrence

The Men

I sat to listen to each sound
Of leaf on twig or ground
And finch that cracked a seed
Torn from a limp and tarnished weed
And rapid flirt of wings
As bluetits flew and used as swings
The bines of old man's beard,
When suddenly I heard
Those men come crashing through the wood
And voices as they stood,
And dog that yelped and whined
At each shrill scent his nose could find;
And knowing that it meant small good
To some of us who owned that wood,
Badger, stoat, rabbit, rook and jay
And smoky dove that clattered away,
Although no ill to me at least,
I too crept off like any stealthy beast.

Andrew Young

Enigma machine

Stammering is like typing a beautifully worded letter, full
of feeling and expression - but when you print it out it is
totally changed. The words are different, *scrambled*, as if
by an enigma machine - and only you know the code.
People follow the fragments of the text - but the essence,
the wholeness, has gone - broken up by hesitations,
blocks, mumbles and deafening pauses.

Some days my speech is a one round fight and I win.
Other days it's a longer contest.
I feel I am winning - but it's hard, tiring, scary
and it always leaves me bruised and fatigued.

Terry McElhinney

Dumb Insolence

I'm big for ten years old
Maybe that's why they get at me

Teachers, parents, cops
Always getting at me

When they get at me

I don't hit 'em
They can do you for that

I don't swear at them
They can do you for that

I stick my hands in my pockets
And stare at them

And while I stare at them
I think about sick

They call it dumb insolence

They don't like it
But can't do you for it

Adrian Mitchell

Reflections at Dawn

I wish I owned a Dior dress
  Made to my order out of satin.
I wish I weighed a little less
  And could read Latin,
Had perfect pitch or matching pearls,
  A better head for street directions,
And seven daughters, all with curls
  And fair complexions.
I wish I'd tan instead of burn.
  But most, on all the stars that glisten,
I wish at parties I could learn
  To sit and listen.

I wish I didn't talk so much at parties.
It isn't that I want to hear
My voice assaulting every ear,
Uprising loud and firm and clear
  Above the cocktail clatter.
It's simply, once a doorbell's rung,
  (I've been like this since I was young)
Some madness overtakes my tongue
  And I begin to chatter.

Buffet, ball, banquet, quilting bee,
  Wherever conversation's flowing,
Why must I feel it falls on me
  To keep things going?
Though ladies cleverer than I
  Can loll in silence, soft and idle,
Whatever topic gallops by,
  I seize its bridle,
Hold forth on art, dissect the stage,
  Or babble like a kindergart'ner
Of politics till I enrage
  My dinner partner.

I wish 1 didn't talk so much at parties.
When hotly boil the arguments,
Ah! would I had the common sense
To sit demurely on a fence
  And let who will be vocal,
Instead of plunging in the fray
With my opinions on display
Till all the gentlemen edge away
  To catch an early local.

Oh! there is many a likely boon
  That fate might flip me from her griddle.
I wish that I could sleep till noon
  And play the fiddle,
Or dance *a tour jete so* light
  It would not shake a single straw down.
But when I ponder how last night
  I laid the law down,
More than to have the Midas touch
  Or critics' praise, however hearty,
I wish I didn't talk so much,
I wish I didn't talk so much,
I wish I didn't talk so much
  When I am at a party.

Phyllis McGinley

"There was nothing wrong with her that a vasectomy of the vocal chords (sic) wouldn't fix"
Lisa Alther, 1976, Kinflicks Ch 4 (DC)

An Old English Nun's Prayer

Lord, Thou knowest better than I know myself that I am growing older and will some day be old. Keep me from the fatal habit of thinking I must say something on every subject and on every occasion.

Release me from craving to straighten out everybody's affairs. Make me thoughtful but not moody; helpful but not bossy. With my vast store of wisdom it seems a pity not to use it all, but Thou knowest Lord that I want a few friends at the end.

Keep my mind from the recital of endless details; give me wings to get to the point. Seal my lips on aches and pains. They are increasing, and love of rehearsing them is becoming sweeter as the years go by. I dare not ask for grace enough to enjoy the tales of other's pains, but help me to endure them with patience.

I dare not ask for improved memory, but for a growing humility and a lessening cocksureness when my memory seems to clash with the memories of others. Teach me the glorious lesson that occasionally I may be mistaken.

Keep me reasonably sweet. I do not want to be a Saint - some of them are so hard to live with - but a sour old person is one of the crowning works of the devil. Give me the ability to see good things in unexpected places and talents in unexpected people. And give me, 0 Lord, the grace to tell them so.

AMEN

Anon

Tullynoe: Tête-à-Tête in the Parish Priest's Parlour

'Ah, he was a grand man.'
'He was: he fell out of the train going to Sligo.'
'He did: he thought he was going to the lavatory.'
'Her did: in fact he stepped out the rear door of the train.'
'He did: God, he must have got an awful fright.'
'He did: he saw that it wasn't the lavatory at all.'
'He did: he saw that it was the railway tracks going away from him.'
'He did: I wonder if . . . but he was a grand man.'
'He was: he had the most expensive Toyota you can buy.'
'He had: well, it was only beautiful.'
'It was: he used to have an Audi.'
'He had: as a matter of fact he used to have two Audis.'
'He had: and then he had an Avenger.'
'He had: and then he had a Volvo.'
'He had: in the beginning he had a lot of Volkses.'
'He had: he was a great man for the Volkses.'
'He was: did he once have an Escort?'
'He had not: he had a son a doctor.'
'He had: he had a Morris Minor too.'
'He had: and he had a sister a hairdresser in Kilmallock.'
'He had: he had another sister a hairdresser in Ballybunion.'
'He had: he was put in a coffin which was put in his father's cart.'
'He was: his lady wife sat on top of the coffin driving the donkey.'
'She did: Ah, but he was a grand man.'
'He was: he was a grand man ..
'Good night, Father.'
'Good night, Mary.'

Paul Durcan

Busy Day

Pop in
pop out
pop over the road
pop out for a walk
pop in for a talk
pop down to the shop
can't stop
got to pop?

got to pop?

pop where?
pop what?

well
I've got to pop round
pop up
pop in to town
pop out and see
pop in for tea
pop down to the shop
can't stop
got to pop

got to pop?

pop where?
pop what?

well
I've got to
pop in
pop out
pop over the road
pop out for a walk
pop in for a talk.........

Michael Rosen

Chivvy

Grown-ups say things like:
Speak up.
Don't talk with your mouth full
Don't stare
Don't point
Don't pick your nose
Sit up
Say please
Less noise
Shut the door behind you
Don't drag your feet
Haven't you got a hankie?

Take your hands out of your pockets
Pull your socks up
Stand up straight
Say thank you
Don't interrupt
No one thinks you're funny
Take your elbows off the table

Can't you make your *own*
mind up about anything?

Michael Rosen

Two Old Ladies Overheard in Totnes

awful when it happens to someone so young
   so young
It's a terrible thing
        terrible thing
terrible
You don't know what to say, do you
   You don't know what to say
Cos really and truly there's nothing you can say is there
       No there's nothing

If a thing is worth having, it's worth waiting for

Adrian Mitchell

Silence

There is a silence where hath been no sound,
  There is a silence where no sound may be,
  In the cold grave - under the deep, deep sea,
Or in wide desert where no life is found,
Which hath been mute, and still must sleep profound;
  No voice is hushed - no life treads silently,
  But clouds and cloudy shadows wander free,
That never spoke, over the idle ground:
But in green ruins, in the desolate walls
  Of antique palaces, where Man hath been,
Though the dun fox, or wild hyena, calls,
  And owls that flit continually between,
Shriek to the echo, and the low winds moan,
There the true Silence is, self-conscious and alone.

Thomas Hood

Silence

Silence: one would willingly
Consume it, eat it like bread.
There is never enough. Now,
When we are silent, metal
Still rings upon shuddering
Metal; a door slams; a child
Cries; other lives surround us.

But remember, there is no
Silence within; the belly
Sighs, grumbles, and what is that
Loud knocking, that summoning?
A drum beats, a drum beats. Hear
Your own noisy machine, which
Is moving towards silence.

Edward Lucie-Smith

Night Speech
(for a Shakespeare Festival)

The bright day is done,
and we are for the dark,

but not for death.

We are, as eyelids fall
and night's silk rises,
stalled in our sleep
to watch the written dark,
brighter than day,
rephrase our stuttered past.

This fur-lined hour
makes princes of each wretch
whose day-bed wasted,
points each lax tongue
to daggered brightness
says what we could not say.

Awake, we stumbled; now
dream-darting truth
homes to each flying wish;
and love replays its hand,
aims its dark pinions nobly,
even its treacheries. . .

Night, that renews, re-orders
day's scattered dust,
shake now from sleep's long lips
all we have lost and done,
stars, pearls and leaded tears
on our closed eyes;

and we are for the dark

Laurie Lee

After Long Silence

Speech after long silence; it is right,
All other lovers being estranged or dead,
Unfriendly lamplight hid under its shade,
The curtains drawn upon unfriendly night,
That we descant and yet again descant
Upon the supreme theme of Art and Song:
Bodily decrepitude is wisdom; young
We loved each other and were ignorant.

W B Yeats

Macbeth Act IV Scene 3 Macduff et al

MALCOLM	What's the newest grief?
ROSS	That of an hour's age doth hiss the speaker;
	Each minute teems a new one.
MACDUFF	How does my wife?
ROSS	Why, well.
MACDUFF	And all my children?
ROSS	Well, too.
MACDUFF	The tyrant has not batter'd at their peace?
ROSS.	No, they were well at peace, when I did leave 'em.
MACDUFF	Be not a niggard of your speech. How goes't?
ROSS	When I came hither to transport the tidings,
	Which I have heavily borne, there ran a rumour
	Of many worthy fellows that were out,
	Which was to my belief witness'd the rather,
	For that I saw the tyrant's power afoot.
	Now is the time of help; your eye in Scotland
	Would create soldiers, make our women fight,
	To doff their dire distresses.
MALCOLM	Be't their comfort
	We are coming thither: gracious England hath
	Lent us good Siward and ten thousand men;
	An older and a better soldier none
	That Christendom gives out.
ROSS	Would I could answer
	This comfort with the like. But I have words
	That would be howl'd out in the desert air,
	Where hearing should not latch them.
MACDUFF	What concern they
	The general cause, or is it a fee-grief
	Due to some single breast?
ROSS	No mind that's honest
	But in it shares some woe, though the main part
	Pertains to you alone.
MACDUFF	If it be mine,
	Keep it not from me; quickly let me have it.
ROSS	Let not your ears despise my tongue for ever,
	Which shall possess them with the heaviest sound
	That ever yet they heard.
MACDUFF	H'm, I guess at it.
ROSS	Your castle is surpris'd, your wife and babes
	Savagely slaughter'd: to relate the manner
	Were on the quarry of these murder'd deer
	To add the death of you.

MALCOLM	Merciful heaven!
	What, man, ne'er pull your hat upon your brows.
	Give sorrow words; the grief that does not speak
	Whispers the o'erfraught heart, and bids it break.
MACDUFF	My children too?
ROSS	Wife, children, servants, all
	That could be found.
MACDUFF	And I must be from thence?
	My wife kill'd too?
ROSS	I have said.
MALCOLM	Be comforted.
	Let's make us medicines of our great revenge
	To cure this deadly grief.
MACDUFF	He has no children. All my pretty ones?
	Did you say all? 0 hell-kite! All?
	What, all my pretty chickens, and their dam
	At one fell swoop?
MALCOLM	Dispute it like a man.
MACDUFFP	I shall do so;
	But I must also feel it as a man:
	I cannot but remember such things were,
	That were most precious to me. Did heaven look on,
	And would not take their part? Sinful Macduff,
	They were all struck for thee. Naught that I am,
	Not for their own demerits, but for mine,
	Fell slaughter on their souls: heaven rest them now!
MALCOLM	Be this the whetstone of your sword, let grief
	Convert to anger: blunt not the heart, enrage it.
MACDUFF	0, I could play the woman with mine eyes
	And braggart with my tongue! But gentle heavens
	Cut short all intermission; front to front
	Bring thou this fiend of Scotland and myself,
	Within my sword's length set him. If he 'scape,
	Heaven forgive him too.
MALCOLM	This tune goes manly.
	Come, go we to the king. Our power is ready;
	Our lack is nothing but our leave. Macbeth
	Is ripe for shaking, and the powers above
	Put on their instruments. Receive what cheer you may:
	The night is long that never finds the day.

William Shakespeare

King John Act III Scene 4   Constance

CONSTANCE　　　　　　　　Grief fills the room up of my absent child,
　　　　　　　　　　　　Lies in his bed, walks up and down with me,
　　　　　　　　　　　　Puts on his pretty looks, repeats his words,
　　　　　　　　　　　　Remembers me of all his gracious parts,
　　　　　　　　　　　　Stuffs out his vacant garments with his form.
　　　　　　　　　　　　Then have I reason to be fond of grief?
　　　　　　　　　　　　Fare you well; had you such a loss as I,
　　　　　　　　　　　　I could give better comfort than you do.
　　　　　　　　　　　　I will not keep this form upon my head, *[Tears her hair]*
　　　　　　　　　　　　When there is such disorder in my wit.
　　　　　　　　　　　　O Lord! my boy, my Arthur, my fair son!
　　　　　　　　　　　　My life, my joy, my food, my all the world !
　　　　　　　　　　　　My widow-comfort, and my sorrows' cure!

William Shakespeare

A Performance of Henry V at Stratford-upon-Avon

Nature teaches us our tongue again
And the swift sentences came pat. I came
Into cool night rescued from rainy dawn.
And I seethed with language — Henry at
Harfleur and Agincourt came apt for war
In Ireland and the Middle East. Here was
The riddling and right tongue, the feeling words
Solid and dutiful. Aspiring hope
Met purpose in "advantages" and "He
That fights with me today shall be my brother."
Say this is patriotic, out of date.
But you are wrong. It never is too late

For nights of stars and feet that move to an
Iambic measure; all who clapped were linked,
The theatre is our treasury and too,
Our study, school-room, house where mercy is

Dispensed with justice. Shakespeare has the mood
And draws the music from the dullest heart:
This is our birthright, speeches for the dumb
And unaccomplished. Henry has the words
For grief and we learn how to tell of death
With dignity. "All was as cold" she said
"As any stone" and so, we who lacked scope
For big or little deaths, increase, grow up
To purposes and means to face events
Of cruelty, stupidity. I walked
Fast under stars. The Avon wandered on
"Tomorrow and tomorrow". Words aren't worn
Out in this place but can renew our tongue,
Flesh out our feeling, make us apt for life.

Elizabeth Jennings

From **Poetry**

And it was at the age ... Poetry arrived
in search of me. I don't know, I don't know where
it came from, from winter or a river.
I don't know how or when,
no, they were not voices, they were not
words, nor silence,
but from a street I was summoned,
from the branches of night,
abruptly from the others.
among violent fires
or returning alone,
there I was without a face
and it touched me.

(Translated by Alastair Reid)

From **La Poesia**

Y fue a esa edad ... Llegó la poesia
a buscarme. No sé, no sé de dónde
salió, de invierno o río.
No sé cómo ni cuándo,
no, no eran voces, no eran
palabras, ni silencio,
pero desde una calle me llamaba,
desde las ramas de la noche,
de pronto entre los otros,
entre fuegos violentos
o regresando solo,
allí estaba sin rostro
y me tocaba.

Pablo Neruda

"Don't look at me in that tone of voice- it tastes a funny colour."
overheard at the greengrocers by Michael Rosen

A Classroom

The day was wide and that whole room was wide,
The sun slanting across the desks, the dust
Of chalk rising. I was listening
As if for the first time,
As if I'd never heard our tongue before,
As if a music came alive for me.
And so it did upon the lift of language,
A battle poem, *Lepanto*. In my blood
The high call stirred and brimmed.
I was possessed yet coming for the first
Time into my own
Country of green and sunlight,
Place of harvest and waiting
Where the corn would never all be garnered but
Leave in the sun always at least one swathe.
So from a battle I learnt this healing peace,
Language a spell over the hungry dreams,
A password and a key. That day is still
Locked in my mind. When poetry is spoken
That door is opened and the light is shed,
The gold of language tongued and minted fresh.
And later I began to use my words,
Stared into verse within that classroom and
Was called at last only by kind inquiry
"How old are you?" "Thirteen"
"You are a thinker". More than thought it was
That caught me up excited, charged and changed,
Made ready for the next fine spell of words,
Locked into language with a golden key.

Elizabeth Jennings

Now winter nights enlarge

Now winter nights enlarge
  The number of their houres,
And clouds their stormes discharge
  Upon the ayrie towres,
Let now the chimneys blaze
  And cups o'erflow with wine:
Let well-tun'd words amaze
  With harmonie divine.
Now yellow waxen lights
  Shall waite on hunny Love,
While youthfull Revels, Masks, and Courtly sights,
  Sleepes leaden spels remove.

This time doth well dispence
  With lovers long discourse;
Much speech hath some defence,
  Though beauty no remorse.
All doe not all things well;
  Some measures comely tread;
Some knotted Ridles tell;
  Some Poems smoothly read.
The Summer hath his joyes,
  And Winter his delights;
Though Love and all his pleasures are but toyes,
  They shorten tedious nights.

Thomas Campion

Piano

Softly, in the dusk, a woman is singing to me
Taking me back down the vista of years, till I see
A child sitting under the piano, in the boom of the
    tingling strings
And pressing the small, poised feet of a mother who
    smiles as she sings.

In spite of myself, the insidious mastery of song
Betrays me back, till the heart of me weeps to belong
To the old Sunday evenings at home, with winter
    outside
And hymns in the cosy parlour, the tinkling piano our
    guide.

So now it is vain for the singer to burst into clamour
With the great black piano appassionato. The glamour
Of childish days is upon me, my manhood is cast
Down in the flood of remembrance, I weep like a child
    for the past.

D H Lawrence

On a Lady Singing Lawes's Music
to Milton's Ode on the Nativity

I closed my eyes, and heard your voice recall,
  Your delicate voice, exact and small and pure,
Each lovely curve and cunning interval,
  Obeying his command with instinct sure:
But caught no echo of that thunderous hymn
  From Zion's walls, where stand in burning row
The ranks of rainbow-winged Seraphim,
Who loud their long uplifted trumpets blow.

Zion was silent: and I only heard
  As 'twere in dawn's dim twilight, in a wood,
The faint sweet music of a hidden bird
  Singing a private joy, not understood
By me, but strangely comforting to me,
From the deep heart of some invisible tree.

J.C.Squire

The Fair Singer

To make a final conquest of all me,
Love did compose so sweet an enemy,
In whom both beauties to my death agree,
Joining themselves in fatal harmony;
That while she with her eyes my heart does bind,
She with her voice might captivate my mind.

I could have fled from one but singly fair:
My disentangled soul itself might save,
Breaking the curlèd trammels of her hair.
But how should I avoid to be her slave,
Whose subtle art invisibly can wreath
My fetters of the very air I breath?

It had been easy fighting in some plain,
Where victory might hang in equal choice;
But all resistance against her is vain,
Who has the advantage both of eyes and voice;
And all my forces needs must be undone,
She having gainèd both the wind and sun.

Andrew Marvell

The Shout

We went out
into the school yard together, me and the boy
whose name and face

I don't remember. We were testing the range
of the human voice:
he had to shout for all he was worth,

I had to raise an arm
from across the divide to signal back
that the sound had carried.

He called from over the park — I lifted an arm.
Out of bounds,
he yelled from the end of the road,

from the foot of the hill,
from beyond the look-out post of Fretwell's Farm —
I lifted an arm.

He left town, went on to be twenty years dead
with a gunshot hole
in the roof of his mouth, in Western Australia.

Boy with the name and face I don't remember,
you can stop shouting now, I can still hear you.

Simon Armitage

Everyone Sang

Everyone suddenly burst out singing;
And I was filled with such delight
As prisoned birds must find in freedom,
Winging wildly across the white
Orchards and dark-green fields; on – on – and out of sight

Everyone's voice was suddenly lifted;
And beauty came like the setting sun:
My heart was shaken with tears; and horror
Drifted away ... O, but Everyone
Was a bird; and the song was wordless; the singing will never be done.

Siegfried Sassoon

The Quartette

Tom sang for joy and Ned sang for joy and old Sam sang for
  joy;
All we four boys piped up loud, just like one boy;
All the ladies that sate with the Squire — their cheeks were all
  wet,
For the noise of the voice of us boys, when we sang our Quartette.

Tom he piped low and Ned he piped low and old Sam he piped
  low;
Into a sorrowful fall did our music flow;
And the ladies that sate with the Squire vowed they'd never forget
How the eyes of them cried with delight, when we sang our
  Quartette.

Walter De La Mare

The Frog Who Dreamed She Was An Opera Singer

There once was a frog
who dreamed she was an opera singer.
She wished so hard she grew a long throat
and a beautiful polkadot green coat
and intense opera singer's eyes.
She even put on a little weight.
But she couldn't grow tall.
She just couldn't grow tall.
She leaped to the Queen Elizabeth Hall,
practising her aria all the way.
Her voice was promising and lovely.
She couldn't wait to leapfrog on to the stage.
What a presence on the stage!
All the audience in the Queen Elizabeth Hall,
gasped to see one so small sing like that.
Her voice trembled and swelled
and filled with colour.
That frog was a green prima donna.

Jackie Kay

To sing out sometimes

Everyone needs to sing out sometimes
out of their stillness
madly as mountains;
wildly as rainstorms spilling their contents
into the chance of the wind;

strange as the fanfares'
coloured grimaces
like faces lit by bonfires;
solo and only
as a valley trapped lake.

Yesterday cut me.
To-morrow won't own me.
In the rich glitter of cities I am lost
and the roaring machine
never goes asleep.

Everyone needs to sing out always
not on platforms
but down the dark tunnels, the echoing alleys,
over the water, at the end of the causeway.

Out of their oneness,
curses or praises
everyone needs to sing and shout
as dawning birds etch sharp noises
to bring themselves back out of the night.

Adrian Campbell

Poem found on a photocopier…

God picks up the reed-flute
world and blows.

Each note is a reed coming
through one of us
a passion
a longing pain.

Remember the lips
Where the wind-breath
originated,
and let your note be clear.
Don't try to end it.
Be your note.

I'll show you how its enough.
Go up on the roof at night,
in this city of soul.
Let everyone climb on their roofs
and sing their notes!

Sing loud!

Rumi (died in 1273)
(Translated by Coleman Banks)

An Epigram on Scolding

Great Folks are of a finer Mold;
Lord! how politely they can scold;
While a coarse *English* Tongue will itch,
For Whore and Rogue; and Dog and Bitch.

Jonathan Swift

Mary the Cook-Maid's Letter to Dr. *Sheridan*

Well; if ever I saw such another Man since my Mother bound my
 Head,
You a Gentleman! marry come up, I wonder where you were
 bred?
I am sure such Words does not become a Man of your Cloth,
I would not give such Language to a Dog, faith and troth.
Yes; you call'd my Master a Knave: Fie Mr. *Sheridan*, 'tis a Shame
For a Parson, who shou'd know better Things, to come out with
 such a Name.
Knave in your Teeth, Mr. *Sheridan*, 'tis both a Shame and a Sin,
And the Dean my Master is an honester Man than you and all
 your kin:
He has more Goodness in his little Finger, than you have in your
 whole Body,
My Master is a parsonable Man, and not a spindle-shank'd hoddy
 doddy.
And now whereby I find you would fain make an Excuse,
Because my Master one Day in anger call'd you Goose.

Jonathan Swift

A Glass of Beer

The lanky hank of a she in the inn over
   there
Nearly killed me for asking the loan of a
   glass of beer;
May the devil grip the whey-faced slut by
   the hair,
And beat bad manners out of her skin for
   a year.

That parboiled ape, with the toughest jaw
   you will see
On virtue's path, and a voice that would
   rasp the dead,
Came roaring and raging the minute she
   looked at me,
And threw me out of the house on the
   back of my head!

If I asked her master he'd give me a cask
   a day;
But she, with the beer at hand, not a gill
   would arrange!
May she marry a ghost and bear him a
   kitten, and may
The High King of Glory permit her to get
   the mange.

James Stephens

Watch Your French

When my mum tipped a panful of red-hot fat
Over her foot, she did quite a little chat,
And I won't tell you what she said
But it wasn't:
"Fancy that !
I must try in future to be far more careful
With this red-hot scalding fat!"

When my dad fell over and landed—splat!—
With a trayful of drinks (he'd tripped over the cat)
I won't tell you what he said.
But it wasn't:
"Fancy that !
I must try in future to be far more careful
To step *round* our splendid cat!"

When Uncle Joe brought me a cowboy hat
Back from the States, the dog stomped it flat,
And. I won't tell you what I said.
But Mum and Dad yelled:
"STOP THAT!
Where did you learn that appalling language?
Come on. Where?"

"I've no idea," I said,
"No idea."

Kit Wright

"Loquacity, n. A disorder which renders the sufferer unable to curb his tongue
when you wish to talk."

Ambrose Bierce, 1911, The Devil's Dictionary (DC)

Babbling and Gabbling

My Granny's an absolute corker,
My Granny's an absolute cracker,
But she's Britain's speediest talker
And champion yackety-yacker!

Everyone's fond of my Granny,
Everyone thinks she's nice,
But before you can say Jack Robinson,
My Granny's said it twice !

Kit Wright

"You know you haven't stopped talking since I came here? You must have been vaccinated with a phonograph needle."
Groucho Marx, 1933, character in Duck Soup, film script by Bert Kalmer et al (DC)

Father and I in the Woods

'Son,'
My father used to say,
'Don't run.'

'Walk,'
My father used to say,
'Don't talk.'

'Words,'
My father used to say,
'Scare birds.'

So be:
It's sky and brook and bird
And tree.

David McCord

Waiting for the Tone

My sister is my surest friend
And yet, GREAT SNAKES! she seems to spend
Her *life* upon the telephone
Talking to her boyfriend, Tone,
Although — a sad and sorry joke —
She doesn't seem to *like* the bloke.

'Don't take that tone with me, Tone,
Don't take that tone with me,
Or else I'll put down the phone, Tone,
And alone, Tone, you will be.

'Don't call me just to moan, Tone,
Can't stand your whingeing on.
Next time you ring for a groan, Tone,
You'll find that l have gone.'

And she can keep this up for hours:
Her taste for Tone's moans never sours.
So when I think that he might call
I silently steal down the hall
And give the phone a hateful look . . .
Then take the blighter off the hook.

Kit Wright

The Tempest Act III Scene 2   Caliban

CALIBAN   Be not afeard; the isle is full of noises,
             Sounds, and sweet airs, that give delight and hurt not.
             Sometimes a thousand twangling instruments
             Will hum about mine ears; and sometime voices
             That, if I then had waked after long sleep,
             Will make me sleep again; and then, in dreaming,
             The clouds methought would open, and show riches
             Ready to drop upon me, that when I waked
             I cried to dream again.

William Shakespeare

The Listeners

'Is there anybody there?' said the Traveller,
  Knocking on the moonlit door;
And his horse in the silence champed the grasses
  Of the forest's ferny floor:
And a bird flew up out of the turret,
  Above the Traveller's head:
And he smote upon the door again a second time;
  'Is there anybody there?' he said.
But no one descended to the Traveller;
  No head from the leaf-fringed sill
Leaned over and looked into his grey eyes,
  Where he stood perplexed and still.
But only a host of phantom listeners
  That dwelt in the lone house then
Stood listening in the quiet of the moonlight
  To that voice from the world of men:
Stood thronging the faint moonbeams on the dark stair,
  That goes down to the empty hall,
Hearkening in an air stirred and shaken
  By the lonely Traveller's call.
And he felt in his heart their strangeness,
  Their stillness answering his cry,
While his horse moved, cropping the dark turf,
  'Neath the starred and leafy sky;

For he suddenly smote on the door, even
  Louder, and lifted his head:--
'Tell them I came, and no one answered,
  That I kept my word,' he said.
Never the least stir made the listeners,
  Though every word he spake
Fell echoing through the shadowiness of the still house
  From the one man left awake:
Ay, they heard his foot upon the stirrup,
  And the sound of iron on stone,
And how the silence surged softly backward,
  When the plunging hoofs were gone.

Walter de la Mare

Nothing

He thought he heard
A footstep on the stair,
'It's nothing,' he said to himself,
'Nothing is there.'
He thought then he heard
A snuffling in the hall,
'It's nothing; he said again,
'Nothing at all.'
But he didn't open the door
In case he found nothing
Standing there.
On foot or tentacle or paw.
Timidly quiet he kept to his seat
While nothing stalked the house
On great big feet.
It was strange though
And he'd noticed this
When on his own before,
Nothing stalked throughout the house
But never through his door.
The answer he thought,
Was very plain. It was because there was nothing there -
Again!

Julie Holder

The Telephone

'When I was just as far as I could walk
From here today,
There was an hour
All still
When leaning with my head against a flower
I heard you talk.
Don't say I didn't, for I heard you say —
You spoke from that flower on the windowsill —
Do you remember what it was you said?'

'First tell me what it was you thought you heard.'

'Having found the flower and driven a bee away,
I leaned my head,
And holding by the stalk,
I listened and I thought I caught the word —
What was it? Did you call me by my name?
Or did you say —
Someone said "Come" — I heard it as I bowed.'

'I may have thought as much, but not aloud.'

'Well, so I came.'

Robert Frost

Song of the Battery Hen

We can't grumble about accommodation:
we have a new concrete floor that's
always dry, four walls that are
painted white, and a sheet-iron roof
the rain drums on. A fan blows warm air
beneath our feet to disperse the smell
of chicken-shit and, on dull days,
fluorescent lighting sees us.

You can tell me: if you come by
the North door, I am in the twelfth pen
on the left-hand side of the third row
from the floor; and in that pen
I am usually the middle one of three.
But, even without directions, you'd
discover me. I have the same orange-
red comb, yellow peak and auburn
feathers, but as the door opens and you
hear above the electric fan a kind of
one-word wail, I am the one
who sounds loudest in my head.

Listen. Outside this house there's an
orchard with small moss-green apple
trees; beyond that, two fields of
cabbages; then, on the far side of
the road, a broiler house. Listen:
one cockerel crows out of there, as
tall and proud as the first hour of sun.
Sometimes I stop calling with the others
to listen, and wonder if he hears me.

The next time you come here, look for me.
Notice the way I sound inside my head.
God made us all quite differently.
and blessed us with this expensive home.

Edwin Brock

'Tis the Voice of the Lobster

"'Tis the voice of the Lobster: I heard him declare
"You have baked me too brown, I must sugar my hair."
As a duck with its eyelids, so he with his nose
Trims his belt and his buttons, and turns out his toes.
When the sands are all dry, he is gay as a lark,
And will talk in contemptuous tones of the Shark:
But, when the tide rises and sharks are around,
His voice has a timid and tremulous sound.'

Lewis Carroll

Quarrel

He says to me, he says,
D'you want a thick ear? he says.
Who? I says.
You! He says
Me? I says.
Yes, he says.

I says, Oooh.

Traditional

From **Leaves of Grass**

O what is it in me that makes me tremble so at voices?
Surely whoever speaks to me in the right voice, him or
     her I shall follow,
As the water follows the moon, silently, with fluid steps
     anywhere around the globe.

All waits for the right voices ;

…For I see every word utter'd thence has deeper, sweeter,
     new sounds, impossible on less terms.

I see brains and lips closed, tympans and temples
     unstruck,
Until that comes which has the quality to strike and to
     unclose,
Until that comes which has the quality to bring forth
     what lies slumbering forever ready in all words.

Walt Whitman

"To expect to rule others by assuming a loud tone is like thinking oneself tall by
putting on high heels."

J. Petit-Senn (Conceits & Caprices)

Memories of Christmas
from Quite Early One Morning

I remember that we went singing carols once, a night or two before
Christmas Eve, when there wasn't the shaving of a moon to light
the secret, white-flying streets. At the end of a long road was a drive
that led to a large house, and we stumbled up the darkness of the
drive that night, each one of us afraid, each one holding a stone in
his hand in case, and all of us too brave to say a word. The wind
made through the drive-trees noises as of old and unpleasant and
maybe web-footed men wheezing in caves. We reached the black
bulk of the house.

'What shall we give them?' Dan whispered.

'Hark the Herald? 'Christmas comes but Once a Year?'

'No,' Jack said, 'We'll sing "Good King Wenceslas". I'll count three.'

One, two, three, and we began to sing, our voices high and
seemingly distant in the snow-felted darkness round the house
that was occupied by nobody we knew. We stood close together,
near the dark door.

> Good King Wenceslas looked out
> On the Feast of Stephen.

And then a small, dry voice, like the voice of someone who has
not spoken for a long time, suddenly joined our singing: a small,
dry voice from the other side of the door: a small, dry voice through
the keyhole. And when we stopped running we were outside *our*
house; the front room was lovely and bright; the gramophone was
playing; we saw the red and white balloons hanging from the gas-
bracket; uncles and aunts sat by the fire; I thought I smelt our supper
being fried in the kitchen. Everything was good again, and
Christmas shone through all the familiar town.

Dylan Thomas

Cousin Janice with the Big Voice

When my cousin Janice
Opens her mouth to speak
A storm kindles behind her teeth
And a gale pours out.
This is a voice used
To holding conversations
With cows and sheep and dogs
Across mountains and valleys
But here across the tablecloth
In our small flat
When she asks for the sugar
The teacups tremble
And a tidal wave foments
In the eddies of the cherry trifle.

Gareth Owen

Aunt Julia

Aunt Julia spoke Gaelic
very loud and very fast.
I could not answer her -
I could not understand her.

She wore men's boots
when she wore any.
- I can see her strong foot,
stained with peat,
paddling the treadle of the spinningwheel
while her right hand drew yarn
marvellously out of the air.

Hers was the only house
where I've lain at night
in the absolute darkness
of a box bed, listening to
crickets being friendly.

She was buckets
and water flouncing into them.
She was winds pouring wetly
round house-ends.
She was brown eggs, black skirts
and a keeper of threepenny bits
in a teapot.

Aunt Julia spoke Gaelic
very loud and very fast.
By the time I had learned
a little, she lay
silenced in the absolute black
of a sandy grave
at Luskentyre.
But I hear her still, welcoming me
with a seagull's voice
across a hundred yards
of peatscrapes and lazybeds
and getting angry, getting angry
with so many questions
unanswered.

Norman MacCaig

Words

Words, smoothly spoken like the wind,
suddenly hit a wall.
No way round.
Block

Words, flowing like the gently rippling sea are
suddenly uneven and jerky -
as waves, ever repeating.
Repetition

Words, normally like a limp elastic band
suddenly get s t r e t c h e d until
it twangs back into shape.
Prolongation

The silent wall.-
the endless waves -
the tightening band -
all come together to form the unspeakable
STAMMER.

Naomi Lewis, aged 12 years

From **Nicholas Nickleby**

"KATE, my dear," said Mrs. Nickleby; "I don't know how it is, but a fine warm summer day like this, with the birds singing in every direction, always puts me in mind of roast pig, with sage and onion sauce and made gravy."

"That's a curious association of ideas, is it not, mamma?"

"Upon my word, my dear, I don't know," replied Mrs. Nickleby. "Roast pig -- let me see. On the day five weeks after you were christened, we had a roast -- no, that couldn't have been a pig, either, because I recollect there were a pair of them to carve, and your poor papa and I could never have thought of sitting down to two pigs—they must have been partridges. Roast pig! I hardly think we ever could have had one, now I come to remember, for your papa could never bear the sight of them in the shops, and used to say that they always put him in mind of very little babies, only the pigs had much fairer complexions; and he had a horror of little babies, too, because he couldn't very well afford any increase to his family, and had a natural dislike to the subject. It's very odd now, what can put that in my head! I recollect dining once at Mrs. Bevan's, in that broad street, round the corner by the coachmaker's, where the tipsy man fell through the cellar-flap of an empty house nearly a week before quarter-day, and wasn't found till the new tenant went in—and we had roast pig there. It must be that, I think, that reminds me of it, especially as there was a little bird in the room that would keep on singing all the time of dinner -- at least, not a little bird, for it was a parrot, and he didn't sing exactly, for he talked and swore dreadfully; but I think it must be that. Indeed I am sure it must. Shouldn't you say so, my dear?"

Charles Dickens

"The opposite of talking isn't listening. The opposite of talking is waiting."
Fran Lebowitz, 1981, People in Social Studies (DC)

Upon Julia's Voice

So smooth, so sweet, so silv'ry is thy voice,
As, could they hear, the Damn'd would make no noise.
But listen to thee, (walking in thy chamber)
Melting melodious words, to Lutes of Amber.

Robert Herrick

"Voices - I think they must go deeper into us than other things. I have often fancied heaven might be made of voices."

George Eliot

The Solitary Reaper

BEHOLD her, single in the field,
  Yon solitary Highland Lass!
Reaping and singing by herself;
  Stop here, or gently pass!
Alone she cuts and binds the grain,
And sings a melancholy strain;
0 listen! for the Vale profound
Is overflowing with the sound.

No Nightingale did ever chaunt
  More welcome notes to weary bands
Of travellers in some shady haunt,
  Among Arabian sands:
A voice so thrilling ne'er was heard
In spring-time from the cuckoo-bird,
Breaking the silence of the seas
Among the farthest Hebrides.

Will no one tell me what she sings?—
  Perhaps the plaintive numbers flow
For old, unhappy, far-off things,
  And battles long ago:
Or is it some more humble lay,
Familiar matter of to-day?
Some natural sorrow, loss or pain,
That has been, and may be again?

Whate'er the theme, the maiden sang
  As if her song could have no ending;
I saw her singing at her work,
  And o'er the sickle bending;—
I listened, motionless and still;
  And, as I mounted up the hill,
The music in my heart I bore,
Long after it was heard no more.

William Wordsworth

From **The Idea of Order at Key West**

> It was her voice that made
> The sky acutest at its vanishing.
> She measured to the hour its solitude.
> She was the single artificer of the world
> In which she sang. And, when she sang, the sea,
> Whatever self it had, became the self
> That was her song, for she was the maker. Then we,
> As we beheld her striding there alone,
> Knew that there never was a world for her
> Except the one she sang; and, singing, made.

Wallace Stevens

From **Under The Net**

From Proust we were led on to discuss what it meant to describe a feeling or a state of mind. Hugo found this very puzzling, as indeed he found everything very puzzling.

"There's something fishy about describing people's feelings," said Hugo. "All these descriptions are so dramatic."

"What's wrong with that?" I said

"Only," said Hugo, "that it means that things are falsified from the start. If I say afterwards that I felt such and such, say that I felt 'apprehensive'—well, this just isn't true."

"What do you mean ?" I asked.

"I didn't feel this," said Hugo. "I didn't feel anything of that kind at the time at all. This is just something I say afterwards."

"But suppose I try hard to be accurate," I said.

"One can't be," said Hugo. "The only hope is to avoid saying it. As soon as I start to describe, I'm done for. Try describing anything, our conversation for instance, and see how absolutely instinctively you . . . "

"Touch it up ?" I suggested.

"It's deeper than that," said Hugo. "The language just won't let you present it as it really was."

"Suppose then," I said, "that one were offering the description at the time."

"But don't you see," said Hugo, "that just gives the thing away. One couldn't give such a description at the time without seeing that it was untrue. All one could say at the time would be perhaps something about one's heart beating. But if one said one was apprehensive this could only be to try to make an impression—it would be for *effect*, it would be a lie."

I was puzzled by this myself. I felt that there was something wrong in what Hugo said, and yet I couldn't see what it was. We discussed the matter a bit further, and then I told him, "But at this rate almost everything one says, except things like 'Pass the marmalade' or 'There's a cat on the roof', turns out to be a sort of lie."

Hugo pondered this. "I think it is so," he said with seriousness.

"In that case one oughtn't to talk," I said.

"I think perhaps one oughtn't to," said Hugo, and he was deadly serious. Then I caught his eye, and we both laughed enormously, thinking of how we had been doing nothing else for days on end.

"That's colossal !" said Hugo. "Of course one does talk. But," and he was grave again, "one does make far too many concessions to the need to communicate."

"What do you mean?"

"All the time when I speak to you, even now, I'm saying not *precisely* what I think, but what will impress you and make you respond. That's so even between us—and how much more it's so where there are stronger motives for deception. In fact, one's so used to this one hardly sees it. The whole language is a machine for making falsehoods."

"What would happen if one *were* to speak the. truth?" I asked. "Would it be possible?"

"I know myself," said Hugo, "that when I really speak the truth the words fall from my mouth absolutely dead, and I see complete blankness in the face of the other person."

"So we never really communicate ?"

"Well," he said, "I suppose *actions* don't lie."

Iris Murdoch

On The Road Home

It was when I said,
"There is *no* such thing as the truth,"
That the grapes seemed fatter.
The fox ran out of his hole.

You. . . You said,
"There are many truths,
But they are not parts of a truth."
Then the tree, at night, began *to* change,

Smoking through green and smoking blue.
We were *two* figures in a wood.
We said we stood alone.

It was when I said,
"Words are not forms of a single word.
In the sum of the parts, there are only the parts.
The world must be measured by eye";

It was when you said,
"The idols have seen lots of poverty,
Snakes and gold and lice,
But not the truth";

It was at that time, that the silence was largest
And longest, the night was roundest,
The fragrance of the autumn warmest,
Closest and strongest.

Wallace Stevens

From **Alias Grace**

It was difficult to begin talking. I had not talked very much for over fifteen years... and in a way I had forgotten how. I told Dr. Jordan that I did not know what he wanted me to say. He said it wasn't what he wanted me to say, but what I wanted to say myself, that was of interest to him. I said I had no wants of that kind, as it was not my place to want to say anything...

Then let us discuss the weather; he said, you must have some observations he said to make on it, since that is the way everyone else begins.

I smiled at that, but I was just as shy. I was not used to having my opinion asked, even about the weather, and especially by a man with a notebook. The only men of that kind I ever encountered were Mr Kenneth MacKenzie, Esq., the lawyer, and I was afraid of him: and those in the court room at the trial, and in the jail; and they were from the newspapers, and made up lies about me.

Since I could not talk at first, Dr. Jordan talked himself. He told me about how they were building railroads everywhere now, and how they laid down the tracks, and how the engines worked, with the boiler and the steam. This had the effect of setting me more at my ease; and I said I would like to ride in a railway train like that; and he said that perhaps someday I would. I said I did not think so, being sentenced here for life, but then you never can tell what time will have in store for you....

Then I was sad, as I remembered that I would never be married now, or have any babies of my own, though there can be too much of a good thing you could say, and I would not like to have nine or ten and then die of it, as happens to many. But still it is a regret.

When you are sad it is best to change the subject. I asked if he. had a mother living, and he said yes, although her health was not good; and I said that he was fortunate to have a mother living, as mine was not. And then I changed the subject again, and said I was very fond of horses, and he told me about his horse Bess, that he had as a boy. And after a time, I don't know how it was, but little by little I found I could talk to him more easily, and think up things to say.

And that is how we go on. He asks a question, and I say an answer, and he writes it down. In the courtroom, every word that came out of my mouth was as if burnt into the paper they were writing it on, and once I said a thing I knew I could never get the words back; only they were the wrong words, because whatever I said would be twisted around, even if it was the plain truth in the first place. And it was the same with Dr. Bannerling at the Asylum.

But now I feel as if everything I say is right. As long as I say something, anything at all, Dr. Jordan smiles and writes it down, and tells me I am doing well.

While he writes, I feel as if he is drawing me; or not drawing me, drawing on me — drawing on my skin. — not with the pencil he is using, but with an old-fashioned goose pen, and not with the quill end but with the feather end. As if hundreds of butterflies have settled all over my face, and are softly opening and closing their wings.

But underneath that is another feeling, a feeling of being wide-eyed awake and watchful. It's like being wakened suddenly in the middle of the night, by a hand over your face, and you sit up with your heart going fast, and no one is there. And underneath that is another feeling still, a feeling like being torn open; not like a body of flesh, it is not painful as such, but like a peach; and not even torn open, but too ripe and splitting open of its own accord.

And inside the peach there's a stone.

Margaret Attwood

"Language never deceives, if only we know how to question it aright."
                    Richard Chenevix Trench, 1851, from Lecture 4 (DC)

Hair Today, No Her Tomorrow

I'VE BEEN upstairs,' she said.
'Oh yes?' I said.
'I found a hair,' she said.
'A hair?' I said.
'In the bed,' she said.
'From a head?' I said.
'It's not mine,' she said.
'Was it black?' I said.
'It was,' she said.
'I'll explain,' I said.
'You swine,' she said.
'Not quite,' I said.
'I'm going,' she said.
'Please don't,' I said.
'I hate you!' she said.
'You do?' I said.
'Of course,' she said.
'But why?' I said.
'That black hair,' she said.
'A pity,' I said.

'Time for truth,' she said.
'For confessions?' I said.
'Me too,' she said.
'You what?' I said.
'Someone else,' she said.
'Oh dear,' I said.
'So there!' she said.
'Ah well,' I said.
'Guess who?' she said.
'Don't say,' I said.
'I will,' she said.
'You would,' I said.
'Your friend,' she said.
'Oh damn,' I said.
'And his friend,' she said.
'Him too?' I said.
'And the rest,' she said.
'Good God,' I said.

'What's that?' she said.
'What's what?' I said.
'That noise?' she said.
'Upstairs?' I said.
'Yes,' she said.
'The new cat,' I said.
'A cat?' she said.
'It's black,' I said.
'Black?' she said.
'Long-haired,' I said.
'Oh no,' she said.
'Oh yes,' I said.
'Oh shit!' she said.
'Goodbye,' I said.
'I lied,' she said.
'You lied?' I said.
'Of course,' she said.

'About my friend?' I said.
'Y-ess,' she said.
'And the others?' I said.
'Ugh,' she said.
'How odd,' I said.
'I'm forgiven?' she said.
'Of course,' I said.
'I'll stay?' she said.
'Please don't,' I said.
'But why?' she said.
'I lied,' I said.
'About what?' she said.
'The new cat,' I said.
'It's white,' I said.

Brian Patten

Careless Listener Regrets,

When God gave out brains,
I thought He said trains,
and I missed mine.
When God gave out looks,
I thought He said books,
and I didn't want any.
When God gave out noses,
I thought He said roses,
and l asked for a red one.
When God gave out legs,
I thought He said kegs,
and I ordered two fat ones.
When God gave out ears,
I thought He said beers,
and I ordered two long ones.
When God gave out chins,
I thought He said gins,
and I ordered a double.
When God gave out heads,
I thought He said beds,
and I asked for a soft one.
God, am I a mess!

Edith Scharff:

From **The Letters of Ted Hughes**

In 1977, Ted Hughes wrote to his teenage daughter, Frieda, commenting on a story she had written::

(1) <u>Remember</u>: when you get to one of those sticky patches—for instance, bottom paragraph on page 1—the best thing, <u>always</u>, is to break it up into small units. Make each small unit interesting & vital in itself. Not necessarily by descriptive detail—maybe by <u>dramatic juxtaposition</u>. And make it brief.

That's a thing to practise: <u>dramatic juxtaposition</u>.

(2) When you get to a sticky passage it may be sticky because <u>it doesn't really belong.</u> That whole first page, for instance, doesn't really belong. It bores you.

Sometimes, in your writing, you get too closely interested, and involved, with something that's not really necessary to the story. Watch that. It always produces a tangled bit of careless writing.

(3) Imagine reading the story to a listener. Always imagine your listener. Then you'll feel instantly where something is too much, & doesn't fit.

You'd also realise, very often, how <u>little</u> it needs to convey quite a big piece of the narrative.

(4) <u>Most important</u> (1) Practise—just a paragraph at a time—copying writing, as I showed you that evening. Raymond Carver is good—because he's simple, clear, & very dramatic. And probably right for you. And you like him. (2) <u>Practise</u> reading aloud. Take a Carver story and read it—quietly to yourself, but aloud—as if to a listener. <u>Read every sentence as a separate musical speech unit.</u> Nothing will teach you more thoroughly to recognise sharp writing. Clean effective sentences.

Don't be too dismayed by all my corrections. Once you've grasped the dramatic shape of your sentences <u>(by reading aloud)</u> and recognised the difference between sharp and dull in language, you'll be very far on.

Love, Daddy (I have spent thousands of hours reading aloud)

Ted Hughes

Hamlet Act III Scene 2

HAMLET Speak the speech, I pray you, as I pronounc'd it to you, trippingly on the tongue; but if you mouth it as many of your players do, I had as lief the town-crier spoke my lines; nor do not saw the air too much with your hand thus, but use all gently, for in the very torrent, tempest, and, as I may say, whirl-wind of your passion, you must acquire and beget a temperance, that may give it smoothness. 0, it offends me to the soul to hear a robustious periwig -pated fellow tear a passion to tatters, to very rags, to to split the ears of the groundlings, who for the most part are capable of nothing but inexplicable dumb-shows, and noise: I would have such a fellow whipp'd for o'erdoing Termagant; it out-herods Herod: pray you, avoid it.

FIRST PLAYER I warrant your honour.

HAMLET Be not too tame neither, but let your own discre-tion be your tutor, suit the action to the word, the word to the action, with this special observance, that you o'erstep not the modesty of nature: for anything so o'erdone is from the purpose of playing, whose end, both at the first, and now, was and is, to hold as 'twere the mirror up to nature, to show virtue her {own} feature, scorn her own image, and the very age and body of the time his form and pressure. Now this overdone, or come tardy off, though it makes the unskilful laugh, cannot but make the judicious grieve, the censure of which one must in your allowance o'erweigh a whole theatre of others. 0, there be players that I have seen play, and heard others praise, and that highly, not to speak it profanely, that neither having the accent of Christians, nor the gait of Christian, pagan, nor man, have so strutted and bellow'd, that I have thought some of nature's journeymen had made men, and not made them well, they imitated humanity so abominably.

FIRST PLAYER I hope we have reform'd that indifferently with us.

HAMLET   O, reform it altogether; and let those that play
your clowns speak no more than is set down for
them: for there be of them that will themselves
laugh, to set on some quantity of barren spectators
to laugh too, though in the mean time some necessary
question of the play be then to be consider'd: that's
villainous, and shows a most pitiful ambition in the
fool that uses it. Go, make you ready.

William Shakespeare

Unemployable

" I usth thu work in the thircusth,"

He said,

Between the intermittent showers that emerged
from his mouth.

" Oh," I said, " what did you do ? "

" I usth thu catcth bulleth in my theeth."

Gareth Owen

At the Musical Festival

'He gev it Wigan!' we'd say long ago
When our loved local baritone,
Rendering *The Erl King* or *Ruddier than the Cherry*,
Hurled his voice like an iron quoit
Clean into the Adjudicator's.
Union-Jacked box at the back. Never mind
If he was out of tune or muddled his words
Or finished bars ahead of the accompanist—
He'd won his marks, he'd done
What he set out to do; he'd
Given it Wigan.

              The map of England
Was a small one then. London
Was Wembley; Blackpool was holidays;
Manchester was the Test:
All else, a blurred and hachured diagram
Of dialects and geology. We chose
Our bench-marks and points of reference within day-return
Of the one place we knew. It was
Barrow for ships, Whitehaven for coal,
Millom, of course, for men,
And Wigan for a damned good try.

So when, apprehensively, I
Go up for my last class and adjudication—the hall packed,
The audience tense, the examining pencil
Slanted on the unmarked sheet—then,
As I huff and grate and fill my lungs, and eye
The once-for-all starting bell,
God grant me guts to die
Giving it Wigan.

Norman Nicholson

Judging Distances

Not only how far away, but the way that you say it
Is very important. Perhaps you may never get
The knack of judging a distance, but at least you know
How to report on a landscape: the central sector,
The right of arc and that, which we had last Tuesday,
    And at least you know

That maps are of time, not place, so far as the army
Happens to be concerned - the reason being,
Is one which need not delay us. Again, you know
There are three kinds of tree, three only, the fir and the poplar,
And those which have bushy tops to; and lastly
    That things only seem to be things.

A barn is not called a barn, to put it more plainly,
Or a field in the distance, where sheep may be safely grazing.
You must never be over-sure. You must say, when reporting:
At five o'clock in the central sector is a dozen
Of what appear to be animals; whatever you do,
    Don't call the bleeders *sheep*.

I am sure that's quite clear; and suppose, for the sake of example,
The one at the end, asleep, endeavours to tell us
What he sees over there to the west, and how far away,
After first having come to attention. There to the west,
On the fields of summer the sun and the shadows bestow
    Vestments of purple and gold.

The still white dwellings are like a mirage in the heat,
And under the swaying elms a man and a woman
Lie gently together. Which is, perhaps, only to say
That there is a row of houses to the left of arc,
And that under some poplars a pair of what appear to be humans
    Appear to be loving.

Well that, for an answer, is what we might rightly call
Moderately satisfactory only, the reason being,
Is that two things have been omitted, and those are important.
The human beings, now: in what direction are they,
And how far away, would you say? And do not forget
     There may be dead ground in between.

There may be dead ground in between; and I may not have got
The knack of judging a distance; I will only venture
A guess that perhaps between me and the apparent lovers
(Who, incidentally, appear by now to have finished)
At seven o'clock from the houses, is roughly a distance
     Of about one year and a half.

Henry Reed

"Do you hate a fashionable voice? I remember, once, asking a now deceased cousin
of mine for a description of some woman. He replied: 'Oh, an empty sardine tin on
a sandy shore' "

Edith Sitwell, Selected Letters, 1919 - 1964

The Oxford Voice

WHEN you hear it languishing
and hooing and cooing and sidling through the front
  teeth,
       the oxford voice
        or worse still
     the would-be oxford voice
you don't even laugh any more, you can't.

For every blooming bird is an oxford cuckoo nowadays,
you can't sit on a bus nor in the tube
but it breathes gently and languishingly in the back of
  your neck.

And oh, so seductively superior, so seductively
       self-effacingly
       deprecatingly
       superior.-
We wouldn't insist on it for a moment
      but we are
     we are
   you admit we are
     superior. —

DH Lawrence

"Uncross your legs dear - I can't hear what you are saying!"
          Elsie Fogerty, Central School of Speech and Drama

Listen Mr Oxford don

Me not no Oxford don
me a simple immigrant
from Clapham Common
I didn't graduate
I immigrate

But listen Mr Oxford don
I'm a man on de run
and a man on de run
is a dangerous one

I ent have no gun
I ent have no knife
but mugging de Queen's English
is the story of my life

I dont need no axe
to split up yu syntax
I dont need no hammer
to mash up yu grammar

I warning you Mr Oxford don
I'm a wanted man
and a wanted man
is a dangerous one

Dem accuse me of assault
on de Oxford dictionary
imagine a concise peaceful man like me
dem want me serve time
for inciting rhyme to riot
but I tekking it quiet
down here in Clapham Common

I'm not a violent man Mr Oxford don
I only armed wit mih human breath
but human breath
is a dangerous weapon

So mek dem send one big word after me
I ent serving no jail sentence
I slashing suffix in self-defence
I bashing future wit present tense
and if necessary

I making de Queen's English accessory to my offence

John Agard

From **Joyce Grenfell Requests the Pleasure**

So cramped were conditions at Clear View that Mrs Alvey's lessons on Friday afternoons had to be given in the Science Lab, and the Science Lab was really the conservatory, built on to the side of the house. There, among the Bunsen burners, I breathed and exercised my voice in duet with Mrs Alvey. At first glance she was hardly suited to teach the subject. Not only was she deaf but she was a cockney with adenoids. There she stood, short and thickset, with a blob of a nose and grey hair in an imprisoning Ena Sharples hairnet, teaching me to use my diaphragm as a bellows. She told ofgifted pupils whose stomach-muscles were so fully developed that with a single intake and release of breath they could send a grand piano rolling across the room.

   We did vocal exercises together. Deep breath; then, starting on a low note, she began: 'Adjels and bidisters of Grace defend us.' She moved up a tone. 'Adjels and bidisters of Grace defend us,' and so on up the scale, teaching us to articulate clearly on the slowly released breath. Mrs Alvey, who didn't wear a corset, invited her pupils to feel the iron discipline of her stomach-muscles by pressing as hard as they could on the beige inserted panel of her long plum-brown princess-line dress. She relied on Shakespeare to develop our vocal techniques. 'The quality of bercy is dot strain'd,' she boomed, and I boomed after her. I was allowed to choose my own recitations and overacted in Jean Ingelow's *High Tide on the Coast of Lincolnshire*. I felt worldly and bitter in *The Forsaken Merman*. These recitations were rendered with intensity and not one glimmer of humour.

Joyce Grenfell

Yellow Butter

Yellow butter purple jelly red jam black bread
Spread it thick
Say it quick
Yellow butter purple jelly red jam black bread
Spread it thicker
Say it quicker
Yellow butter purple jelly red jam black bread
Now repeat it
While you eat it
Yellow butter purple jelly red jam black bread
Don't talk with your mouth full!

Mary Ann Hoberman

From **Imitations of Horace**

"Of little use the Man you may suppose,
Who says in verse what others say in prose;
Yet let me show, a Poet's of some weight,
And, (tho' no soldier) useful to the state.
What will a child learn sooner than a song?
What better teach a foreigner the tongue?
What's long or short, each accent where to place,
And speak in public with some sort of grace?
Yes sir, reflect, the mischief is not great,
These madmen never hurt the church or State;
Sometimes the folly benefits mankind;
And rarely avarice taints the tuneful mind.
Allow him but his plaything of a pen,
He ne'er rebels or plots, like other men;
Flights of cashiers, or mobs, he'll never mind;
And knows no losses while the Muse is kind.
Behold the hand that wrought a nation's cure,
Stretch'd to relieve the idiot and the poor,
Proud vice to brand, or injured worth adorn,
And stretch the ray to ages yet unborn.

Alexander Pope

Herb the Superb's Hound the Sound Poem

Hells bells! What a hubbub
Hotchpotch, hubble bubble!
Here we go, hugger mugger
Hurtle down the helter skelter.

    Hairy canary
    (much too scary)

Habdabs and heeby jeebies
Hanky panky! Hoity toity
Hoi polloi, hurly burly
Honky tonk, burdy gurdy

    Hi 'n' dri
    (wish I could fly)

Hustle 'n' bustle, hurry 'n' scurry
Hither 'n' thither, hickory dickory
Hocus pocus, hippety hoppety
harum scarum, Higgledy piggledy

    Huff 'n' puff
    (that's enuff)

Cicely Herbert

The Six O'Clock News

This is thi
six a clock
news thi
man said n
thi reason
a talk wia
BBC accent
iz coz yi
widny wahnt
me ti talk
aboot thi
trooth wia
voice lik
wanna yoo
scruff, if
a toktaboot
thi trooth
lik wanna yoo
scruff yi
widny thingk
it wuz troo.
jist wanna yoo
scruff tokn.
thirza right
way ti spell
ana right way
ti tok it. this
is me tokn yir
right way a
spellin. this
is ma trooth.
yooz doan no
thi trooth
yirseltz cawz
yi canny talk
right. this is
the six a clock
nyooz. belt up.

Tom Leonard

102

From **Education**

In going through Plato and Demosthenes, since I could now read these authors, as far as the language was concerned, with perfect ease, I was not required to construe them sentence by sentence, but to read them aloud to my father, answering questions when asked: but the particular attention which he paid to elocution (in which his own excellence was remarkable) made this reading aloud to him a most painful task.

   Of all things which he required me to do, there was none which I did so constantly ill, or in which he so perpetually lost his temper with me. He had thought much on the principles of the art of reading, especially the most neglected part of it, the inflections of the voice, or *modulation* as writers on elocution call it (in contrast with *articulation* on the one side, and *expression* on the other), and had reduced it to rules, grounded on the logical analysis of a sentence. These rules he strongly impressed upon me, and took me severely to task for every violation of them; but I even then remarked (though I did not venture to make the remark to him) that though he reproached me when I read a sentence ill, and *told* me how I ought to have read it, he never, by reading it himself, *showed* me how it ought to be read. A defect running through his otherwise admirable modes of instruction, as it did through all his modes of thoughts, was that of trusting too much to the intelligibleness of the abstract, when not embodied in the concrete. . . .

John Stuart Mill

Society Small Talk or what to say and when to say it
From a Victorian Book

'Voice' and 'manner' are of paramount importance in the art of conversing. It is a very erroneous idea to suppose that men or women in fashionable society', or what is termed the 'best society', or 'good society', speak with a lisp or a languid drawl, or with any mannerism whatever. Well-bred people speak in a natural and unaffected manner, the cadence of the voice being low and the intonation thoroughly distinct, each syllable of each word being clearly pronounced, but without pedantry or exaggeration.

The modulation of the tones of the voice is also a great point with the well-educated; and this it is which gives to the voice the slow, measured ring which the uninitiated endeavour to imitate by the assuming an affected drawl, or by speaking in deep and guttural accents, as foreign to the genuine voice of the well-bred man or woman as is the dialect of a Lancashire operative. When ladies speak in deep contralto tones it is because Nature has endowed them with deep contralto voices, and not with an idea of assuming tones other than their natural ones.

The voice is one of the best and truest indications of education and refinement, and betrays the absence of these qualities with almost painful intensity.

Those who possess unrefined or common voices, should, on becoming aware of the fact — and there is no surer way of gaining this knowledge than by comparing the tones of their own uncultivated voices with the tones of more refined ones — endeavour to remedy this defect by clearly *educating* their voices by speaking slowly, clearly, and distinctly, and by pitching the voice in a low key, chest notes are an advantage to persons having 'shrill' voices if they can be made use of without gruffness; thus, with a due regard to accentuation, modulation, and pronunciation, a very fair result may be achieved.

The common error with the many is their rapid or, so to say, slovenly manner of speaking; the slurring over of the final syllables, the dropping of the voice before the words have been half-uttered, and the running a string of words together with hurried ungraceful accents, too often starting with a jerk and concluding with a rush.

Letters from the Lower City,
From Letter number 14

I have been working in a drama school for many years. Very often I listen to the voices of my students so hard that my ears start to ache. I have been trying to sneak inside the sounds they produce and look around them as if they were spacious rooms.

As you probably know voice is one of the realms where the soul can stay. I have always been thinking that body and soul must live as one. For them to live separately is quite extravagant and unnatural.

Most of the troubles I have encountered in my career have been associated with the students who do not want to show their souls to the world, whereas the acting profession, simply **means** flaunting one's naked soul out there in the open. Some souls barely heave in sight, while both the director and the theatre audience want to see them in all their splendour.

My job is to seize such resistant souls by the sounds they produce and simply drag them out for the whole world to see. Then I catch another sound and another, and after a few years, when the work is running well, the soul can perform freely and audibly even in front of the most demanding audience.

Krzysztof Gedroyc
(Translated by Jadwiga Wozniak)

From **Tea at Gunters**

I didn't know anything about elocution teachers and the image I'd made for myself was of someone bustling and efficient—a sort of gymnast of the vocal cords; the reality of Miss Lister however, was something quite other. Her first words to me as she stood dramatically on her front door step, were, 'You are Lucy!' spoken in a deep, vibrating voice. Then repeating, 'You are *Lucy*,' with a sweeping gesture, she led me inside.

Tall and horse-faced, dressed in a tight black silk blouse, her brown cobwebby hair piled up high, she struck awe into me at once. As we walked through the hall, the hem of her long velvet skirt trailing along the linoleum, she said in a sad tone, 'Pupils should arrive at least ten minutes before their lesson is due. Where is your breath, Lucy?' Her own as she leant towards me, smelt of violet cachoux.

The room she was to teach me in was large and dark with a lot of heavy drapes of the same plum-coloured velvet as her skirt. While she asked me some questions about myself, I sat on the edge of a knobbly sofa and gazed for reassurance at a stuffed canary in an ornate wicker cage; she herself sat very upright in a high, carved chair, shuddering as I spoke.

'So flat!' she said. 'Such *slovenly* sounds.'

My vowels, she explained to me sadly were the ugly vowels of Yorkshire townsfolk - never, never of course to be confused with the lovely, country dialect. 'I often sit, quite quietly,' she said, 'on my beautiful visits to the Dales, listening, listening to the shepherd, the ploughman, the herdsman, the —' She searched for another example, but not finding it she waved her arm airily. 'Their dialect is sacred,' she declared. 'I would never tamper with it.'

But my vowels, it appeared, weren't ready for improvement yet: I would have to begin with breathing. Breathing was of the greatest importance; and for what seemed an age, I had to sit before a large diagram showing me in red and black the whole complex of larynx, pharynx, lungs, windpipe, while Miss Lister, blowing violet over me, pointed them all out. Then we did some simple exercises which I was to continue faithfully at home, fifteen minutes every evening. In the meantime we would approach the vowels by stealth as it were, forcing them through beautiful poetry. To this end, I read aloud from the *Golden Treasury*; Miss Lister wincing at regular intervals.

In the middle of *The Lotos-Eaters*, she interrupted me.

'Do you ever go up on the moors, Lucy?' she asked.

'Well, yes,' I said, starting. 'Sometimes. In the summer.'

She stood up suddenly.

106

'Emily Bronte!' she cried. She threw back her arms, straining the buttons of her blouse. Then in her most dramatic voice, she announced, 'Lucy, next time you are up on the moors—I want you to run. Run, run, flinging your arms wide like this,' she made another wild gesture, 'run away, away! Call out your vowels, Lucy. All, ah, ah!' She sounded in pain. 'Hear the wind catch them—a wonderful, rising, falling, dying-away sound—ah, ah, ah!'

I said that certainly I would see about it, and she sat down again, refreshed.

Pamela Haines

The Voice

Woman much missed, how you call to me, call to me,
Saying that now you are not as you were
When you had changed from the one who was all to me,
But as at first, when our day was fair.

Can it be you that I hear? Let me view you, then,
Standing as when I drew near to the town
Where you would wait for me: yes, as I knew you then,
Even to the original air-blue gown!

Or is it only the breeze, in its listlessness
Travelling across the wet mead to me here,
You being ever dissolved to wan wistlessness,
Heard no more again far or near?

   Thus I; faltering forward,
   Leaves around me falling,
Wind oozing thin through the thorn from norward,
   And the woman calling.

Thomas Hardy

After the Book is Closed

Whether it is the words
  or their meanings,
Or the sounds they make,
  or the way they echo one another;
Or simply the pictures
   they paint in the imagination,
Or the ideas they begin,
  or their rhythms . . .

Whether it is the words
  or their histories,
Their curious journeys
  from one language to the next;
Or simply the shapes they make
  in the mouth –
Tongue and lips moving,
  breath flowing . . .

Whether it is the words
  or the letters used
To spell them, the patterns
  they make on the page;
Or simply the way they call feelings
  into the open
Like a fox seen suddenly in a field
   from a hurrying train . . .

Whether it is the words
  or the spaces between –
The white silences
  among the dark print,
I do not know.
   But I know this: that a poem
Will sing in my mind
  long after the book is closed.

Gerard Benson

Aaaaagh!

Aaaaagh! I screamed
for no
reason
at all.

Martin Doyle

Index of Authors

Index of First Lines

Acknowledgements

The Editor and Trustees of the Voice Care Network UK gratefully acknowledge permission to reproduce the following copyright items in this anthology. We offer our apologies to any copyright holders whom we have been unable to locate.

John Agard: "Listen Mr Oxford don" copyright © 1985 by John Agard, reproduced by kind permission of John Agard, c/o Caroline Sheldon Literary Agency Limited.

Moniza Alvi: "Hindi Urdu Bol Chaal" from "Carrying My Wife," 2000, reprinted by permission of Bloodaxe Books.

Simon Armitage: "The Shout" © Simon Armitage from "The Universal Home Doctor," reprinted by permission of Faber & Faber.

Margaret Attwood: from "Alias Grace," © Margaret Attwood, reprinted by permission of Bloomsbury Press.

Gerard Benson: "After the Book is Closed" from "Evidence of Elephants," by permission of the author.

Edwin Brock: "Song of the Battery Hen" from "Five ways to Kill a Man," published by Enitharmon Press.

Adrian Campbell: title poem from "To Sing Out Sometimes," private publication, by permission of the author.

Ciaran Carson: "Second Language" from "First Language," (1993) by kind permission of the author and The Gallery Press, Loughcrewe, Oldcastle. County Meath, Ireland.

Charles Causley: "I am the song" from "Collected Poems," published by Macmillan, by permission of David Higham Associates.

Billy Collins: "Child Development" from "The Apple that Astonished Paris," Copyright © 1988, 1996 by Billy Collins. Used by permission of the University of Arkansas Press, www.uapress.com.

David Crystal: thanks for some footnote quotes (see DC after entries) from "Words on Words" by David and Hilary Crystal, published by Penguin.

Walter de la Mare: "The Listeners" and "The Quartet" reprinted with thanks to the Literary Trustees of Walter de la Mare and the Society of Authors as their representative.

Martin Doyle: "Aaaaagh" from "This Poem Doesn't Rhyme," edited by Gerard Benson, reprinted by permission of the author.

Joyce Dunbar: "I was trapped inside a marble…I couldn't hear a thing" from "Mundo and the Weather Child," © Heinemann, 1986, with permission of David Higham Associates.

Thanks from the Editor

The editor wishes to give a very warm thank you to the dedicated work force who have made this collaborative anthology happen:

Valerie King, for her diligent research with poems and publishers

Roz Comins, for finding and helping to place so much material and for her enthusiastic encouragement at all times

David Comins, for his technical skills, good taste and experience in making this into a book

Annabel Bosanquet, not only for her patience in obtaining most of the copyright permissions, but especially for her imaginative support as a sounding board. She is the perfect co-editor.

And a warm thank you, too, to **Barry Jackson** for permission to reproduce his painting "Lift Off" on the cover of this book.

Heather Kay

We have found all these organisations very helpful in seeking to find the copyright holders and get their permission to reprint:

Local Libraries across the country.

The Poetry Library, Level 5, Royal Festival Hall, Southbank Centre, Belvedere Road, London SE1 8XX
phone: 020 7921 0943,   fax: 020 7921 0939
web site: www.poetrylibrary.org.uk

The Patent Office, Concept House, Cardiff Road, Newport, South Wales, NP10 8QQ
phone: 01633 814000
web site: www.intellectual.copyright

Writers and Artists Yearbook, A & C Black Publishers Ltd, 37 Soho Square, London W1D 3QZ
phone: 020 7758 0200,   email: enquiries@acblack.com
web site: www.acblack.com

Society of Authors, 84 Drayton Gardens, London SW10 9SB
phone: 020 7373 6642,   email: info@societyofauthors.org
web site: www.societyofauthors.org

Poetry Society, 22 Betterton Street, London WC2H